This book was compiled by Daniel Melehi with the A.I assistance of Inventabot

I0504544

<u>Dedication</u>

I hope this helps all of my wonderful readers achieve all their goals in their business. And I would like to thank my wonderful wife for all of her continued support in all my ventures.

May 7 2023

Contents

Introduction to JavaScript and jQuery............................6

    What is JavaScript?..6

    Benefits of jQuery 7

    Understanding the DOM 7

What is JavaScript? **8**

Chapter 2: Setting Up Your Environment....................**11**

Installing a Code Editor **11**

Downloading and Including jQuery in Your Project........**12**

Browser Developer Tools **13**

Installing a Code Editor **14**

Downloading and Including jQuery in Your Project........**16**

Browser Developer Tools **17**

    The Elements Panel 18

    The Console 18

    The Network Panel 19

Chapter 3: JavaScript Basics.........................**20**

Subchapter 3.1: Variables and Data Types....................**20**

Subchapter 3.2: Conditional Statements **21**

Subchapter 3.3: Loops **21**

Subchapter 3.4: Functions **22**

Variables and Data Types **22**

    Strings...23

    Numbers...23

Booleans...23

Null and Undefined 24

Conditional Statements......................................**24**

Example:..25

Loops **26**

Functions **28**

Chapter 4: jQuery Basics **29**

Subchapter 4.1: Selectors and Filters..............**29**

Subchapter 4.2: Manipulating HTML Elements **30**

Subchapter 4.3: Events and Event Handlers.................**32**

Manipulating HTML Elements **34**

Subchapter 4.3: Events and Event Handlers.................**35**

Chapter 5: Creating Interactive Web Pages.................**37**

Subchapter 5.1: Dynamic Effects with jQuery **38**

Subchapter 5.2: Traversing the DOM.............................**39**

Subchapter 5.3: Animation and Effects.........................**39**

Dynamic Effects with jQuery **40**

Animation and Effects **43**

Chapter 6: Best Practices for Front-End Development ..**45**

Writing Clean and Maintainable Code **45**

1. Naming Conventions and Consistency 45

2. Commenting..46

3. Avoiding Global Variables..................................46

Debugging Techniques **47**

1. Console Logging...47

2. Debugging Tools 47

Performance Optimization **48**

1. Minification and Compression 48

2. Caching 48

3. Image Optimization 49

Writing Clean and Maintainable Code **49**

1. Consistent Formatting and Indentation 50

2. Meaningful Variable and Function Names 50

3. Comment Your Code 50

4. Avoid Global Variables 51

5. Use Object-Oriented Programming (OOP) Principles........51

Debugging Techniques **52**

Performance Optimization **53**

Chapter 7: Advanced Techniques **55**

Subchapter 7.1: AJAX and JSON..................................**55**

Subchapter 7.2: Popular jQuery Plugins....................**56**

Subchapter 7.3: Responsive Web Design with jQuery.....**57**

Subchapter 7.1: AJAX and JSON..................................**58**

Popular jQuery Plugins..**59**

1. Slick...59

2. Select2 60

3. DataTables..60

4. Magnific Popup 61

5. FitText..61

Chapter 1: Introduction to JavaScript and jQuery

Introduction to JavaScript and jQuery

JavaScript and jQuery are two of the most popular web development tools in use today. JavaScript is a programming language that allows developers to create interactive web pages. jQuery is a JavaScript library that simplifies the process of creating dynamic web pages and user interfaces.

What is JavaScript?

JavaScript is a programming language that is used to add interactivity to web pages. It is a client-side language, meaning that it is executed on the user's computer (in the web browser) rather than on the web server. JavaScript can be used for a wide variety of tasks, including form validation, creating interactive user interfaces, and even building entire applications.

Benefits of jQuery

jQuery is a JavaScript library that simplifies the process of creating dynamic web pages and user interfaces. It provides a number of features and functions that make it easier to manipulate the Document Object Model (DOM), handle events, and create animations and effects. By using jQuery, developers can write code more quickly and easily than if they were using raw JavaScript.

Understanding the DOM

The Document Object Model (DOM) is a representation of the current state of a web page. It is created by the web browser as it parses the HTML document and converts it into a tree-like structure. Developers can use JavaScript (or jQuery) to manipulate the DOM and create dynamic web pages that respond to user input and other events. In order to effectively use JavaScript and jQuery, it is important to understand the structure and behavior of the DOM.

WHAT IS JAVASCRIPT?

JavaScript is a programming language that is used to add interactivity to web pages. It is the most popular language for web development and is supported by all modern web browsers. JavaScript allows developers to create dynamic and interactive web pages, enabling users to interact with the content in different ways. JavaScript is a client-side language, meaning that it is executed on the user's browser rather than on the server. JavaScript can be used for a variety of tasks, such as form validation, creating animations, and updating the content of a web page without refreshing the entire page. JavaScript is a powerful language that has evolved over time. Originally created in 1995 by Brendan Eich, JavaScript has gone through many revisions and improvements. Today, it is an essential tool for web development and is used by developers all over the world. Understanding JavaScript is crucial for anyone looking to build interactive and engaging web pages.Benefits of jQuery: jQuery is a lightweight, fast, and feature-rich JavaScript library that has become incredibly popular among web developers in recent years. jQuery simplifies HTML document traversing, event handling, and animation for rapid web development. Some of the main benefits of using jQuery in front-end web development are: 1. Simple and Easy to Use: Unlike traditional JavaScript code, jQuery allows developers to write less code for accomplishing the same effects. It uses a simple syntax that is easy to grasp, even for beginners. 2. Cross-browser Compatibility: jQuery has been designed to work seamlessly across all major web browsers, enabling websites to provide similar user experiences to their visitors, regardless of which browser they are using. 3. Big Community and Support:

jQuery has a large and active community of developers who create plugins, write tutorials and articles, and offer support to those who are learning to use it. 4. Efficient and Fast: jQuery delivers excellent performance, ensuring fast loading times, which is a critical factor for all websites in the age of instant gratification. 5. Increased Productivity: jQuery features an extensive selection of pre-written functions that enable web developers to create advanced web applications quickly. By utilizing the numerous benefits of jQuery, developers can save time, streamline their code, and create reliable and efficient web applications.Understanding the Document Object Model (DOM) is crucial for any front-end web developer. The DOM is an interface that allows JavaScript and other web development languages to access and manipulate the content and structure of a web page. Essentially, the DOM creates a tree-like representation of a web page's HTML and XML code, with each element being a node in the tree. This allows developers to manipulate the content and structure of the page in real-time, without the need for server-side processing. In this subchapter, we will delve deeper into the workings of the DOM. We will discuss how it is constructed, and how it can be accessed and manipulated using JavaScript and jQuery. We will also explore the concept of event-driven programming, where events such as mouse clicks or button presses can trigger changes to the DOM. Whether you are just starting out in web development or are a seasoned pro, a thorough understanding of the DOM is essential for creating responsive and dynamic web pages. So buckle up and get ready to dive into the fascinating world of DOM manipulation!

Chapter 2: Setting Up Your Environment

INSTALLING A CODE EDITOR

Before you can start writing any JavaScript or jQuery code, you need to have a code editor installed on your computer. A code editor is a software application that allows you to write and edit code for web development. There are many code editors available, both free and paid, so it's important to do your research and choose the one that best suits your needs. Some popular code editors include: - **Visual Studio Code**: A free, open-source code editor developed by Microsoft. It's lightweight, fast, and has a large community of developers who create helpful extensions. - **Sublime Text**: A paid code editor that's known for its speed and efficiency. It's highly customizable and has a large library of plugins and extensions. - **Atom**: A free, open-source code editor developed by GitHub. It's highly customizable and has a large library of plugins and extensions. Once you've chosen a code editor, you can start setting it up to work with JavaScript and jQuery.

DOWNLOADING AND INCLUDING JQUERY IN YOUR PROJECT

jQuery is a popular JavaScript library that simplifies the process of working with HTML documents and events. To use jQuery in your project, you first need to download it and include it in your HTML file. There are two ways to include jQuery in your project: 1. Download jQuery from the official website and include it in your HTML file using a `<script>` tag. You can download jQuery from https://jquery.com/download/. 2. Include jQuery in your project using a content delivery network (CDN). A CDN is a system of servers that deliver content, such as JavaScript files, to users based on their geographic location. To use a CDN to include jQuery in your project, you can add the following code to your HTML file: `<script src="https://code.jquery.com/jquery-3.6.0.min.js"></script>` This code will load the latest version of jQuery from the jQuery CDN.

BROWSER DEVELOPER TOOLS

Most modern web browsers, such as Google Chrome and Mozilla Firefox, come with built-in developer tools that allow you to inspect and debug web pages. These tools can be accessed by right-clicking on a web page and selecting "Inspect" or by pressing the F12 key. Some common features of browser developer tools include: - **Element inspection**: You can select any element on a web page to view its HTML markup and CSS styles. - **JavaScript console**: You can execute JavaScript code and view any error messages or console logs. - **Network monitoring**: You can monitor the network traffic of a web page to view details such as response times and HTTP headers. Browser developer tools are an essential part of web development, and mastering them will make your development process much smoother.

INSTALLING A CODE EDITOR

JavaScript and jQuery are two of the most popular tools used in front-end web development. To work with them effectively, you need to have a code editor installed on your computer. A code editor is a software application that lets you write, edit, and manage your code easily and efficiently. There are many code editors available, both free and paid. Some of the popular code editors that you can use for JavaScript and jQuery development include Sublime Text, Atom, Visual Studio Code, and Brackets. Each of these code editors has different features, so you should choose one that best suits your needs and preferences. To install a code editor, you can usually visit the website of the editor you have chosen and download the installer. Once the download is complete, run the installer and follow the prompts to set up the code editor on your computer. It′s a straightforward process, and most code editors come with clear instructions to guide you along the way. Once you have installed a code editor, you can start creating JavaScript and jQuery files, and use the editor to write, edit, and debug your code. Having a good code editor can make your work much easier and more efficient, so take some time to explore the different options and find one that works for you.

DOWNLOADING AND INCLUDING JQUERY IN YOUR PROJECT

jQuery is a powerful tool that can simplify the process of creating dynamic and interactive web pages. In order to use jQuery, you must first download and include it in your project. To download jQuery, simply go to the official website (jquery.com) and click the download button.

You can choose to download the compressed, production version or the uncompressed, development version. The compressed version is recommended for production websites, while the uncompressed version is useful for debugging and development. Once you have downloaded the jQuery file, you can include it in your HTML document using a script tag. The script tag should be placed in the head of your HTML document, or at the bottom of your body to ensure that the page content loads before the script. For example, you can include jQuery in your HTML file by adding the following code: ``` ``` Make sure to replace the "path/to/jquery.min.js" with the actual path to your jQuery file. By including jQuery in your project, you will have access to numerous powerful functions and methods that can help streamline your front-end development process. With this powerful library at your disposal, you can easily manipulate HTML elements, create dynamic animations, and add interactive features to your web pages.

BROWSER DEVELOPER TOOLS

Browser developer tools are essential for front-end web development, and they allow you to inspect, debug, and optimize your code. Modern browsers come with built-in developer tools that you can access by pressing F12 or right-clicking on the page and selecting "Inspect element." In this subchapter, we will explore the main features of browser developer tools, including the elements panel, the console, and the network panel.

The Elements Panel

The elements panel is where you can inspect and manipulate the HTML and CSS of a webpage. By selecting an element, you can see its attributes and styles. You can also modify the HTML and styles and see the changes in real-time. The elements panel also provides a useful tool for debugging layout issues. By hovering over an element, you can see its dimensions and spacing, helping you to identify and fix rendering problems.

The Console

The console is where you can execute JavaScript commands and log messages. This is useful for debugging JavaScript code and for testing new features. You can test expressions and functions, interact with the DOM, and log messages to the console. The console also provides a range of tools for debugging, including breakpoints, stepping through code, and profiling.

The Network Panel

The network panel is where you can monitor the network requests made by your webpage. This includes requests for HTML, CSS, JavaScript, images, and other resources. By inspecting the network panel, you can see how long each request takes, the size of the files, and any errors that occur. This is useful for optimizing the performance of your webpage, as you can identify slow-loading resources and reduce the size of files. In summary, browser developer tools are essential for front-end web development. They provide a range of features for inspecting and manipulating the HTML, CSS, and JavaScript of a webpage, as well as for debugging and optimizing its performance. By mastering these tools, you can become a more efficient and effective web developer.

Chapter 3: JavaScript Basics

JavaScript is a programming language used to create interactive and dynamic web pages. In this chapter, we will cover the fundamental concepts of JavaScript.

SUBCHAPTER 3.1: VARIABLES AND DATA TYPES

Variables are used to store values in JavaScript. Variables can be declared using the 'let' or 'var' keyword, followed by the variable name. There are several data types in JavaScript, including strings, numbers, booleans, null, and undefined. Strings are used to store text, while numbers are used to store numerical values. Booleans can only be either 'true' or 'false', while null and undefined are used to represent empty values.

SUBCHAPTER 3.2:
CONDITIONAL STATEMENTS

Conditional statements are used in JavaScript to make decisions based on certain conditions. The 'if' statement is used to execute code if a certain condition is true, while the 'else' statement is used to execute code if the condition is false. The 'else if' statement can be used to specify another condition if the first one is not met. The 'switch' statement can also be used to specify multiple possible outcomes for a single condition.

SUBCHAPTER 3.3: LOOPS

Loops are used in JavaScript to execute a block of code multiple times. The 'for' loop is used to execute code a specified number of times, while the 'while' loop is used to execute code as long as a certain condition is true. The 'do-while' loop is similar to the 'while' loop, but it always executes the code within the loop at least once.

SUBCHAPTER 3.4: FUNCTIONS

Functions are used in JavaScript to encapsulate reusable pieces of code. Functions are declared using the 'function' keyword, followed by the function name and any parameters. Functions can either return a value or not, depending on what the code within the function does. Functions can also be assigned to variables, allowing them to be passed around as arguments to other functions.

VARIABLES AND DATA TYPES

JavaScript is a dynamic programming language, which means that we do not have to specify a variable's data type when we declare it. Variables can be declared using the "var" keyword. For example, we could declare a variable named "name" like this: ```javascript var name = "John"; ``` In this example, we have assigned a string value of "John" to the variable "name". JavaScript has several data types, including strings, numbers, booleans, null, and undefined. Let's take a closer look at each of these data types:

Strings

Strings are used to represent text in JavaScript. They are enclosed in quotation marks, either single or double. ```javascript var message = "Hello, world!"; ```

Numbers

Numbers are used to represent numeric values in JavaScript. They can be either integer or decimal. ```javascript var age = 27; var price = 14.99; ```

Booleans

Booleans are used to represent true or false values in JavaScript. ```javascript var isCorrect = true; var isActive = false; ```

Null and Undefined

Null and undefined are used to represent the absence of a value. Null is explicitly assigned, while undefined is used for uninitialized variables or non-existent properties. ```javascript var noValue = null; var notDefined; ``` Understanding variables and data types is fundamental to writing effective JavaScript code. In the next subchapter, we will learn about conditional statements and how they can be used to control the flow of our programs.

CONDITIONAL STATEMENTS

In programming, conditional statements are used when you want to execute a code block only if a certain condition is true. JavaScript provides a few key conditional statements that you can use to make decisions in your code. The most commonly used conditional statement is the **if** statement. This statement checks if a certain condition is true and if so, executes a block of code. For example, you might use an if statement to check if a user has entered a password correctly before allowing them to access a secure part of your website. Another useful conditional statement is the **else if** statement, which allows you to specify additional conditions to check if the initial if statement is false. Finally, you can use the **else** statement to specify a block of code to execute if none of the previous conditions are true. Here's an example of how you might use these statements in a function to check the age of a user and determine what message to display:

Example:

```
function checkAge(age) { if (age < 18) {
return "Sorry, you're not old enough to
enter."; } else if (age >= 18 && age < 21) {
return "You can enter, but you can't drink.";
} else { return "You're free to enter and
drink!"; } }
```
In this function, we first check if the user's age is less than 18, in which case we return a message telling them they can't enter. If the age is not less than 18, we move on to the else if statement to check if the user is between 18 and 21. If so, we return a message telling them they can enter but can't drink. Finally, if neither of the previous conditions are true (i.e. the user is 21 or older), we return a message telling them they can enter and drink. Conditional statements are an important part of JavaScript programming and are used in many contexts. Learning how to use them effectively can make your code more efficient and your programs more flexible.

LOOPS

Loops are an essential part of JavaScript programming that allows you to repeat a block of code multiple times. There are different types of loops in JavaScript, but the most commonly used are the "for" loop and the "while" loop. The "for" loop is used when you know how many times you want to repeat a block of code. Here's an example:

```javascript
for (let i = 0; i < 5; i++) {
  console.log("This is iteration number " + i);
}
```

This loop starts with the variable "i" set to 0, runs the code inside the loop as long as "i" is less than 5, and increments "i" by 1 after each iteration. The output of this loop would be:

```
This is iteration number 0
This is iteration number 1
This is iteration number 2
This is iteration number 3
This is iteration number 4
```

The "while" loop is used when you don't know how many times you want to repeat a block of code. Here's an example:

```javascript
let i = 0;
while (i < 5) {
  console.log("This is iteration number "
```

+ i); i++; } ``` This loop starts with the variable "i" set to 0, runs the code inside the loop as long as "i" is less than 5, and increments "i" by 1 after each iteration. The output of this loop is the same as the "for" loop above. Loops are useful for iterating over arrays and manipulating their values. They can also be used to validate user input, perform calculations, and many other tasks. Just remember to always include an exit condition for your loop, or you might end up with an infinite loop that crashes your program!

FUNCTIONS

Functions are an essential part of JavaScript and jQuery programming. A function is a block of code that performs a specific task, just like a variable stores a specific value. The main advantage of using functions is that they can be called multiple times throughout your code without having to rewrite the entire block of code. Here is the basic syntax for creating a function: ```

function functionName(parameter1, parameter2, parameter3) { // block of code to be executed return result; } ``` In the above example, `functionName` is the name of the function, `parameter1`, `parameter2`, and `parameter3` are input parameters that the function can use, and `result` is what the function returns. Keep in mind that the `return` statement is optional and if it is omitted, the function will return `undefined`. Let's take a look at a real example to see how functions are used in practice: ``` function calculateArea(width, height) { var area = width * height; return area; } var rectArea = calculateArea(10, 5); console.log(rectArea); // Output: 50 ``` In the above example, we have defined a function called `calculateArea` that takes in `width` and `height` parameters and calculates the area of a rectangle by multiplying them together. We then use the function by calling it with `calculateArea(10, 5)` and storing the result in `rectArea`. Functions are incredibly versatile and can be used for a wide range of tasks, from simple calculations like the one above, to complex string manipulations, or even making API requests. In the next chapter, we will take a closer look at jQuery and its capabilities for manipulating HTML elements and creating dynamic web pages.

Chapter 4: jQuery Basics

SUBCHAPTER 4.1: SELECTORS AND FILTERS

jQuery makes it a breeze to manipulate HTML elements on a page. But before we can manipulate elements, we need to be able to select them. That's where selectors come in. Selectors allow us to easily target specific HTML elements based on their ID, class, or tag name. Here's an example of how to select an element with a specific ID using jQuery: $('#my-element') This selects the element with the ID "my-element". Filters are another way to further narrow down our selection of elements. The most common filter is the :first filter. Here's an example: $('.my-class: first') This selects the first element with the class "my-class". There's also a : last filter which selects the last element with a specific tag or class name. There are many other filters available in jQuery, which makes it very powerful for selecting and manipulating HTML elements.

SUBCHAPTER 4.2: MANIPULATING HTML ELEMENTS

Now that we know how to select elements with jQuery, let's take a look at how to manipulate them. jQuery has a plethora of methods for manipulating HTML elements, such as changing their text, HTML, or CSS properties. Here's an example of how to change the text of an element: $('#my-element').text('Hello, world!'); This changes the text of the element with ID "my-element" to "Hello, world!". If we want to change the HTML of an element instead of the text, we can use the .html() method instead of .text(). Here's an example: $('#my-element').html('**Hello, world!**'); This changes the HTML of the element with ID "my-element" to "**Hello, world!**". We can also change CSS properties of HTML elements using jQuery. Here's an example of how to change the background color of an element: $('#my-element').css('background-color', 'red'); This changes the background color of the element with ID "my-element" to red.

SUBCHAPTER 4.3: EVENTS AND EVENT HANDLERS

Another powerful feature of jQuery is the ability to add event handlers to HTML elements. An event handler is a function that executes when a specific event occurs, such as user clicking a button. Here's an example of how to add a click event handler to a button with a specific ID: $('#my-button').click(function() { alert('Button clicked!'); }); This adds a click event handler to the button with ID "my-button".

When the button is clicked, an alert box will appear with the message "Button clicked!". There are many other events that can be handled in jQuery, such as mouseenter, mouseleave, and submit. Event handling is a crucial part of creating interactive web pages, and jQuery makes it easy to add event handlers to elements.Selectors are one of the most important features of jQuery. They help to select specific HTML elements from a web page, and apply manipulations and actions to them. jQuery offers a wide range of selectors, from basic element selectors to more complex filter selectors. Element selectors are used to select specific HTML elements based on their tag name. For example, $("p") selects all paragraphs on a web page. ID selectors select elements based on their unique ID attribute. To select an HTML element by its ID, use the "#" symbol followed by the ID name. For example, $("#myHeading") selects the element with the ID "myHeading". Class selectors select all elements with the specified class name. To select HTML elements by class name, use the ".''" symbol followed by the class name. For example, $(".myClass") selects all elements with the class "myClass". Filter selectors are used to refine element selection based on specific criteria. For example, the :first selector selects only the first element, while the :last selector selects only the last element. Additionally, the :even and :odd selectors select every even and odd element, respectively. Overall, the use of selectors and filters play a crucial role in the manipulation of HTML elements with jQuery. They provide an efficient way to target specific elements and apply desired changes.

MANIPULATING HTML ELEMENTS

With jQuery, you can easily manipulate HTML elements using its powerful methods. In this chapter, we will explore some of the most commonly used methods and techniques for manipulating HTML elements. One of the most basic ways to manipulate an HTML element with jQuery is by changing its content. You can do this using the `html()` method. For example, if you want to change the text inside a paragraph element with an id of `my-paragraph`, you can use the following code:

`$('#my-paragraph').html('New text here');` In addition to changing the content of an element, you can also change its attributes using the `attr()` method. For example, if you want to change the source of an image with an id of `my-image`, you can use the following code: `$('#my-image').attr('src', 'new-image-source.jpg');` Another useful method for manipulating HTML elements with jQuery is the `addClass()` method. This method allows you to add a new class to an element. For example, if you want to add a new class of `highlight` to a div element with an id of `my-div`, you can use the following code: `$('#my-div').addClass('highlight');` Similarly, the `removeClass()` method allows you to remove a class from an element. These are just a few examples of the many ways in which you can manipulate HTML elements using jQuery. With these powerful methods at your disposal, you can create dynamic and interactive web pages that engage and delight your users.

SUBCHAPTER 4.3: EVENTS AND EVENT HANDLERS

Events are actions that occur on a web page, such as a user clicking a button or submitting a form. In jQuery, you can use event handlers to create interactive web pages that respond to user actions. One of the most common ways to use events in jQuery is to assign a function to execute when a particular event occurs. For example, you could use the `click()` function to execute a function when a user clicks on a button: ```
$("#myButton").click(function() { alert("Button clicked!"); }); ``` In this example, we're selecting the HTML element with an ID of "myButton" using

jQuery's `$()` function. We're then using the `click()` function to assign an anonymous function that displays an alert message when the button is clicked. jQuery provides a wide range of event handlers that you can use in your web development projects. Here are some of the most common events and event handlers: - `click()` - executes a function when an element is clicked - `submit()` - executes a function when a form is submitted - `mouseover()` - executes a function when the mouse pointer is over an element - `keydown()` - executes a function when a key is pressed down - `keyup()` - executes a function when a key is released In addition to these basic event handlers, jQuery also provides support for delegated events, which allow you to create event handlers for elements that haven't been created yet. This can be especially useful for dynamic web pages that generate content on the fly. Overall, events and event handlers are a powerful tool in jQuery that you can use to make your web pages more interactive and engaging for your users.

Chapter 5: Creating Interactive Web Pages

Creating interactive web pages is one of the core elements of modern web development, and JavaScript and jQuery are powerhouse tools that can help you accomplish this task easily and efficiently. In this chapter, you will learn several techniques for adding interactivity to your web pages using JavaScript and jQuery.

SUBCHAPTER 5.1: DYNAMIC EFFECTS WITH JQUERY

jQuery provides a comprehensive set of methods for creating dynamic effects that can make your web pages more engaging and interactive. Some of the most commonly used effects include fading, sliding, and animating HTML elements. Fading is a simple way to add transitions to page elements. You can make an element fade in or out, or you can adjust its opacity gradually. Sliding effects, on the other hand, allow you to move HTML elements up, down, left, or right based on user interaction. By default, sliding effects use an easing function that gives the animation a more natural look and feel. Animating HTML elements is a more advanced technique that combines fading and sliding effects with other types of animations, such as rotating, scaling, and skewing. Animating elements can make them more eye-catching and can help draw your users' attention to specific parts of your page.

SUBCHAPTER 5.2: TRAVERSING THE DOM

Traversing the Document Object Model (DOM) is an essential technique for working with HTML elements in JavaScript and jQuery. DOM traversal allows you to select HTML elements based on their relationship to other elements on the page. jQuery provides a rich set of methods for traversing the DOM, including parent(), children(), siblings(), and next(). By using these methods, you can select and manipulate specific page elements based on their position relative to other elements on the page.

SUBCHAPTER 5.3: ANIMATION AND EFFECTS

Animation and effects are a powerful way to add interactivity and engagement to your web pages. jQuery provides a range of built-in animation and effect methods that allow you to create everything from simple buttons to complex interactive elements. Some of the most popular animation and effect methods are animate(), slideToggle(), and fadeToggle(). These methods allow you to create dynamic buttons, menus, and even entire interactive features that can help bring your web pages to life. In this section, you will learn how to combine these animation and effect methods with other jQuery techniques, such as event handling and DOM traversal, to create compelling interactive experiences that will keep your users engaged and coming back for more.

DYNAMIC EFFECTS WITH JQUERY

jQuery makes it easy to add dynamic effects and animations to your web pages. With jQuery, you can create interactive and engaging web content that responds to user actions and enhances the user experience. One of the simplest ways to add dynamic effects with jQuery is by using the `.hide()` and `.show()` methods. These methods allow you to hide or show HTML elements on your web page with a smooth and elegant animation. For example, you can hide a `<div>` element when the page loads, and then show it when the user clicks on a button. Another popular jQuery effect is the `.fadeIn()` and `.fadeOut()` methods. These methods gradually fade an HTML element in or out of view, creating a subtle and attractive effect that draws the user's attention. You can use these methods to create eye-catching visuals and add extra flair to your web pages. If you want to create more complex animations, jQuery provides a powerful `.animate()` method that lets you specify custom CSS properties to animate over a period of time. With this method, you can create smooth and fluid animations that respond to user actions and create a memorable user experience. Finally, jQuery also provides methods for creating interactive effects like tooltips and modals. These methods allow you to create dynamic content that responds to user actions, adding an extra layer of interactivity to your web pages. In summary, jQuery provides a wide range of dynamic effects and animations that you can use to enhance your web content and create engaging user experiences. Whether you're hiding and showing elements, fading them in and out, or animating custom CSS properties, jQuery makes it easy to create web pages that are both beautiful and functional. Traversing the DOM is an important skill for any front-end developer, and jQuery makes it easy with a wide array of traversal methods. At its core, DOM traversal is the ability to move up, down, and across the HTML structure of a web page. With jQuery, you can traverse the DOM using selectors, filters, and methods like `.parent()`, `.children()`, and `.siblings()`. `.parent()` allows you to select the direct parent of an element, while `.children()` selects all the direct children of an element. `.siblings()` selects all the siblings of an element. jQuery also provides more powerful traversal methods like `.find()`, which allows you to search for elements within a selected set of elements, and `.next()`, which selects the immediately following sibling of an element. By using these methods and combining them with other jQuery functionalities, you can create powerful and dynamic web pages that respond to user actions and events. In the next chapter, we'll dive deeper into animation and effects with jQuery to enhance the user experience even further.

ANIMATION AND EFFECTS

jQuery provides a range of animation and effect methods that can be used to add visually appealing elements to your website. These animations can help to engage your website visitors and to make your website stand out from the competition. One of the most commonly used animation methods in jQuery is the "animate" method. With the animate method, you can animate specific CSS properties over a given duration. For example, you could use jQuery to animate the opacity of an element, making it fade in or out gradually. Another popular effect in jQuery is the "slide" effect. With this effect, you can make an element slide up or down, or slide in from the left or right. This effect can be used to make dropdown menus or to create a more dynamic user interface. The "toggle" effect is also useful for adding interesting effects to your website. With this effect, you can toggle between two or more states of an element. For example, you could use the toggle effect to show or hide a div on your webpage. Overall, jQuery animations and effects can add a lot of visual interest to your website. However, it's important to use them in moderation and to make sure that they don't detract from the usability of your website. With some careful planning and experimentation, you can create a website that is both visually interesting and user-friendly.

Chapter 6: Best Practices for Front-End Development

WRITING CLEAN AND MAINTAINABLE CODE

As a front-end developer, it is crucial to write code that is easy to read, understand and maintain. Writing clean and maintainable code requires proper organization, consistency, and adherence to best practices. Here are some tips for writing clean and maintainable code:

1. Naming Conventions and Consistency

Use consistent naming conventions for your variables, functions and classes. Descriptive and self-explanatory names will make it easier for other developers to understand your code. Avoid using abbreviations and acronyms that may not be familiar to everyone.

2. Commenting

Adding comments to your code is essential for clear communication with other developers. Comments will help others better understand your code and make it easier to troubleshoot problems. Commenting is especially important to explain why you are doing something, not just what you are doing.

3. Avoiding Global Variables

Avoid using global variables as much as possible. Using too many global variables can lead to name collisions and cause unexpected issues. Instead, use local variables or create functions to encapsulate your code.

DEBUGGING TECHNIQUES

Debugging is a critical part of front-end development. When things go wrong, developers need to have a process for identifying and fixing bugs. Here are some debugging techniques that you can use:

1. Console Logging

Console logging is the simplest and most popular way to debug JavaScript code. Using console.log to debug your code can help you understand what is happening in your code at any moment in time.

2. Debugging Tools

Browser Developer Tools, such as Chrome Developer Tools and Firefox Developer Tools, provide powerful tools for debugging JavaScript code. These tools allow you to use breakpoints, step through your code, and inspect variables.

PERFORMANCE OPTIMIZATION

Fast websites are critical for keeping users engaged and happy. The performance of your front-end code can impact your website's speed. Here are some tips for optimizing your website's performance:

1. Minification and Compression

Minifying and compressing your JavaScript and CSS files can significantly reduce their size and improve your website's loading time. Use tools like UglifyJS and GZIP to minify and compress your files.

2. Caching

Leverage browser caching to improve your website's speed by storing frequently accessed files and data on the user's computer. This can significantly improve the speed of your website.

3. Image Optimization

Images can be the largest assets on a webpage. Optimizing images can reduce their sizes and improve the loading speed of your website. Use tools like Photoshop, TinyPNG, and JPEGmini to optimize your images. Remember, writing clean and maintainable code, effective debugging, and performance optimization are critical for front-end development. By adhering to these best practices, you can develop fast, efficient, and responsive web applications that meet user expectations.

WRITING CLEAN AND MAINTAINABLE CODE

As a developer, writing clean and maintainable code is crucial. Not only does it make your code easier to read and understand, it also makes it easier for others to collaborate and contribute to your project. Here are some tips for writing clean and maintainable JavaScript and jQuery code:

1. Consistent Formatting and Indentation

Consistent formatting and indentation is crucial for code readability. It helps developers quickly understand the structure of the code and navigate through it. Always use the same formatting and indentation style throughout your codebase.

2. Meaningful Variable and Function Names

Use meaningful names for your variables, functions, and classes. Avoid using abbreviated or overly generic names. This makes it easier for other developers to understand your code and collaborate with you.

3. Comment Your Code

Commenting your code is an essential part of writing maintainable code. Comments should be used to explain the purpose and functionality of your code. Only comment code that is not self-explanatory, as too many comments can actually make the code harder to read.

4. Avoid Global Variables

Global variables can create naming conflicts and make it difficult to understand the flow of your code. Use local variables instead, and avoid defining unnecessary global variables.

5. Use Object-Oriented Programming (OOP) Principles

By using OOP principles, you can make your code more organized and easier to understand. Encapsulating functionality within objects helps to reduce the scope of variables and functions, making your code more modular and easier to maintain. Incorporating these tips into your JavaScript and jQuery development will result in clean and maintainable code that can be easily understood and collaborated on by other developers.

DEBUGGING TECHNIQUES

Debugging is an essential part of any development process, and JavaScript and jQuery are no exception. Debugging errors can be frustrating, but it's important to be patient and methodical in order to find and fix the issue. One of the most basic and important tools for debugging is the console. The console allows you to log variables and output messages to help understand the flow of your code and identify any issues. To open the console, right-click on your webpage and select "Inspect" or "Inspect Element". Then, click on the "Console" tab to access the console. Another useful tool is the "debugger" statement. Placing the word "debugger" in your code will pause the execution of your code at that point, allowing you to step through the code and see how it's executing. This can help you identify the root cause of your issue more efficiently. Many code editors also have built-in debugging tools that can be helpful for identifying and fixing errors. These tools allow you to set breakpoints in your code and step through it line by line, so you can see exactly how your code is executing and identify any errors along the way. It's also important to make a habit of writing clean and well-organized code, with clear comments and variable names, to make it easier to track down and fix bugs. And always remember to test your code thoroughly, using different browsers and devices, to ensure that it's functioning properly for all users. By using a combination of these debugging techniques, you can identify and fix any issues in your JavaScript and jQuery code and ensure that your web applications are running smoothly for your users.

PERFORMANCE OPTIMIZATION

In today's fast-paced digital world, it is more important than ever to optimize the performance of your web applications. Slow-loading websites and apps can lead to frustration for users and a decrease in overall engagement. To ensure that your site runs as smoothly and efficiently as possible, it is crucial to focus on performance optimization. One of the best ways to optimize performance is to minimize the amount of data that needs to be transferred between the user's device and your server. This can be accomplished by using techniques such as minifying your CSS and JavaScript files, reducing image sizes, and utilizing compression techniques like gzip. Another important strategy for optimizing performance is to make use of caching. By storing frequently accessed data on the user's device or in their browser cache, you can reduce the amount of time it takes for your site to load. Additionally, enabling browser caching can help reduce server requests and improve response times. JavaScript and jQuery provide a number of tools and techniques that can be used to further optimize performance. For example, you can make use of asynchronous loading techniques to load JavaScript and CSS files in the background, without delaying the loading of other critical resources. You can also use lazy loading to delay the loading of non-critical elements until they are needed, thus improving the initial load time of your site. Ultimately, the key to successful performance optimization is to continually monitor and test your site, making adjustments as needed to ensure optimal performance. This may involve using tools like Google's PageSpeed Insights or YSlow, which can provide insights into areas where your site may be falling short in terms of performance and speed. By focusing on performance optimization, you can improve the user experience for your site visitors and keep them engaged with your content for longer periods of time.

Chapter 7: Advanced Techniques

SUBCHAPTER 7.1: AJAX AND JSON

AJAX (Asynchronous JavaScript and XML) is a technique used in web development to create fast and dynamic web pages. It allows web pages to be updated asynchronously by exchanging data with a web server in the background. JSON

(JavaScript Object Notation) is a lightweight data interchange format. It is easy for humans to read and write, and easy for machines to parse and generate. Most modern web APIs use JSON as their data format. In this section, we will explore how to use AJAX with jQuery and how to work with JSON data in your web applications. We will learn how to send and receive data using AJAX, how to handle errors, how to work with JSON data, and more.

SUBCHAPTER 7.2: POPULAR JQUERY PLUGINS

jQuery has a vast collection of plugins that extend its functionality and help developers to create more advanced and complex web applications. These plugins can be easily integrated into your web applications and can save you a lot of time and effort. In this section, we will explore some of the most popular jQuery plugins available today. We will learn what they do, how to use them, and how to customize them to suit your needs. Some of the plugins we will cover include jQuery UI, Slick, Flot, and DataTables.

SUBCHAPTER 7.3: RESPONSIVE WEB DESIGN WITH JQUERY

Responsive web design is a key technique in modern web development. It allows web pages to adapt to different screen sizes and resolutions, ensuring a consistent and user-friendly experience across devices. In this section, we will explore how jQuery can help you to create responsive web pages. We will learn how to use media queries, breakpoints, and other techniques to create flexible and adaptive layouts. We will also learn how to use jQuery plugins to create responsive navigation menus, image galleries, and more.

SUBCHAPTER 7.1: AJAX AND JSON

AJAX (Asynchronous JavaScript and XML) is a powerful technology that allows web pages to be updated dynamically without having to refresh the entire page. With AJAX, you can make requests to the server in the background and receive data in various formats such as JSON, XML and HTML. However, JSON (JavaScript Object Notation) has become the preferred format for exchanging data between the client and server due to its simplicity, high performance, and compatibility with JavaScript. In this chapter, we will explore how to use AJAX to send and receive JSON data. We'll cover the different AJAX methods provided by jQuery, including the $.ajax(), $.get(), and $.post() methods, and how to handle the AJAX response data. We'll also delve into JSON, and examine how to create and parse JSON data. You'll see how you can use AJAX and JSON together to create powerful and efficient web applications. With AJAX and JSON, you can create dynamic, interactive, and responsive websites that provide a richer user experience. So let's get started and learn how to master AJAX and JSON in your web development projects.

POPULAR JQUERY PLUGINS

One of the main reasons why jQuery is so popular among front-end developers is the vast library of plugins available for use. These plugins are designed to make it easier to implement common functionality, such as image sliders, form validation, and lightboxes. Let's take a look at some of the most popular jQuery plugins that you should consider using in your web development projects:

1. Slick

Slick is a powerful and flexible carousel plugin for jQuery that allows you to create responsive and touch-enabled sliders for your web pages. With Slick, you can customize the appearance, behavior, and functionality of your image slider to suit your needs, and it comes with a large number of configuration options to make your life easier.

2. Select2

Select2 is a replacement for the standard select box that provides a more user-friendly and flexible way to select options from a dropdown menu. It comes with support for searching, tagging, and remote data sources, and is highly customizable, making it a great choice for complex form fields.

3. DataTables

DataTables is a powerful, yet easy-to-use plugin that allows you to display and manipulate large datasets in your web pages. It provides features such as sorting, filtering, pagination, and search, and has a rich API that allows you to customize its behavior to suit your needs.

4. Magnific Popup

Magnific Popup is a responsive, lightweight, and flexible jQuery lightbox plugin that allows you to display images, videos, and other media in a stylish and elegant manner. It comes with a variety of customization options, including different animation effects, fullscreen mode, and support for retina displays.

5. FitText

FitText is a jQuery plugin that makes it easy to create responsive headlines that automatically adjust to fit the size of the container they are in. This is particularly useful for creating headlines that look great on any device, without having to manually adjust the font size or line height. These are just a few examples of the many jQuery plugins available for use in your web development projects. By taking advantage of these plugins, you can save time and effort, while also providing a better user experience for your website visitors.

www.ingramcontent.com/pod-product-compliance
Lightning Source LLC
Chambersburg PA
CBHW070850220526
45466CB00005B/1950